Funeral Pie

FUNERAL PIE

by
Stuart Friebert

FOUR WAY BOOKS
Marshfield

Editorial Office
Four Way Books
PO Box 607
Marshfield, MA 02050

Library of Congress Number 95-061375

ISBN 1-884800-07-6

Cover painting, watercolor by Fulvio Testa, 1985
Text design by Acme Art, Inc.
Manufactured in the United States of America

This book is printed on acid-free paper.

Four Way Books is a division of Friends of Writers, Inc., a Vermont-based not-for-profit organization.

Produced at The Print Center., Inc., 225 Varick St., New York, NY 10014, a non-profit facility for literary and arts-related publications. (212) 206-8465

For Sarah & Stephen

Also By Stuart Friebert

Poetry

Dreaming of Floods
Calming Down
Up in Bed
Stories My Father Can Tell
Uncertain Health
The Darmstadt Orchids
Kein Trinkwasser
Die Prokuristen Kommen
Nicht Hinauslehnen

Prose

Der Gast, Und Sei Er Noch So Schlecht

Translations

Marin Sorescu, *Hands Behind My Back: Selected Poems*
(with Gabriela Dragnea & Adriana Varga)
Miroslav Holub, *Sagittal Section*
(with Dana Habova)
Günter Eich, *Valuable Nail: Selected Poems*
(with David Walker & David Young)
Giovanni Raboni, *The Coldest Year of Grace: Selected Poems*
(with Vinio Rossi)
Karl Krolow, *On Account Of: Selected Poems*
Karl Krolow, *What'll We Do With This Life: Selected Poems 1950-1990*

Anthologies

A Field Guide To Contemporary Poetry & Poetics
(with David Young)
The Longman Anthology of Contemporary American Poetry
(with David Young)
Models of the Universe: An Anthology of the Prose Poem
(With David Young)

Editions

Max Frisch, *Als Der Krieg Zu Ende War*

ACKNOWLEDGEMENTS

Thanks especially to Diane Vreuls and David Young for their deep human support and editorial acumen over the years, and to the editors of the following journals, in which a number of the poems previously appeared, sometimes in different form:

Artful Dodge
Birmingham Poetry Review
The Centennial Review
Confrontation
Context South
Crab Creek Review
Great Stream Review
Harvard Review
Iowa Review
Kiosk
Lost Creek Letters
Manhattan Poetry Review
New England Review
Onthebus
The Quarterly
Santa Monica Review
Scarecrow Poetry Anthology
Sell-Outs
Shenandoah
The Three-Lobed Burning Eye
The Wallace Stevens Journal
Wind Magazine
Witness

CONTENTS

I

II

III

I

Funeral Pie

Usually raisin, with a latticed top,
served right after we finish the last
of the cold ham and chicken. Later, on
the way back home, we stop for another
slice at the Dutch restaurant off the pike.

It's always on the menu, and if you have
a second helping, it's as though you can
suddenly speak a foreign language, say
things which can be made to go with food
after someone dies, someone not necessarily
your mother or father yet, especially your
mother — you stroll back from the restroom,
look at her some more through the smoke.
If you're lucky, there will be one or two
more years left to move closer before it's
her turn, unless, as she herself says, You
die first, something a parent most fears.

For a child to die, she'd look obstinately
into my eyes, Is to drown everything else,
mix violence with love in a way no human
can fathom — and then she'd swipe a piece
of my pie, after getting me to fall for some
bird out the window, which was never there.

Feed Tree

The one out back the possum frequents
for its blackgum, its babies tucked so

far down in her pouch that we only see
a pink nose now and then. It's just as

serious a thing to have babies for them
as it is for us, I tell the children

when they make a joke about those little
runts, turn up their noses. Home from a

long day at the office, I say, It's nice
to be met at the top of the pouch with a

tantalizing odor from below — a little
smell-trail that leads you straight home.

As usual, I don't have the last word. But
dad, Hannah says, You don't eat us the way

the possum sometimes does her own. I saw
that on a PBS Special once. Sure she's got

the facts wrong, I rush to the town library,
start checking. The truth can cause such harm.

Next Cat

Here are some things my daughter and I went over
when she entered the clinic for treatments and I
said I'd be glad to keep her cat, warts and all:

Do you know how to apply artificial respiration?
(To a drowned cat?)

How you get him to drop a bird?
(Throw a stone past his ear?)

Read to him!
(Pour him some brandy too?)

And please don't pull him up by his ears!
(The way President Johnson used to treat
his hounds? I always thought they loved it.)

And talk to him a lot, Dad.
(I'll keep him up nights, don't worry.)

After the first treatment, she's silent a moment.
And here I am, perfectly calm. I said I was calm.

Dickinson's Mare

Around Mt. Tom, we mean a dragonfly
that lights on the tip of your rod,

but we're not so far away from Emily's
that I can't help thinking it's the one

she wished for as a child — so small,
so eager to soar, taking little puffs

of breath God no longer fussed about,
putting out a finger to test the wind.

Searching the sources, I can only find
one mention of a horse and conclude

she never had a heart to heart talk
with the animal that might have led

to something besides that magnificent
pessimism. She was comfortable inside,

though when the fire was lit on stone
in the corner of her room, she'd notice

the air was not good and fresh, not
what the mare might have breathed,

so she breathed more painfully, flung
from her lungs all final words.

On Wigs

We're watching Sophocles in Athens. It's
her first evening out since deciding on
a wig to hide the effects of radiation.

The Greeks got it right. Black wigs for
tyrants, blond for heroes, red for comic
servants. The early Church did its part,

frowned on wigs as evil. Along came Louis
XIII, prematurely bald, so back they came.
From *perruque* to *periwig* to *wig*, we shorten

as we lengthen. In one of our books, I see
the 18th Century produced more than 40 types:
pigeon's wig, comet, spinach seed, artichoke,

wild boar's head, moving freely among flora
and fauna. Some women owned them all in tints.
Shaving off our own hair, donning that of others

is right up there with Pepys, whom we've taken
to reading at this time in our lives. He wore
his own hair for a wig! But I still can't fathom

this: when we confess our sins, you in yours are
more guiltless than the rest of us. God must know
that. I turn back the covers, take you in my arms.

Wait, you say, Nobody kisses me in my wig and you
toss it clear across the room. When you wag your
head, all the world's a stage again, curtain up!

Draw Day

The first Monday of the month,
grampa sent me down for his pay.
Sale day too, so gramma started
pinning her hair up for shopping.

I never made it back with his
check, something about trouble
at the plant I didn't understand,
refused the ration cards they

handed out instead. In my fear,
I took off for the river. Grampa's
a good man, I kept repeating, and
they should have paid him. After

a few minutes of skipping stones,
I fashioned a pole from a branch
and had myself some perch by noon.
I think I cleaned them, wrapped

them in leaves, and said, when
I handed them to gramma, Here's
the roast, new potatoes and green
beans. Can I have cherry pie for

dessert, with milk-coffee, please?
Remember how we say *impossible*
in Hungarian? she said, and took
my face into her apron. Grampa

just stood there, arms limp at
his sides — earlier miseries
coming back like a jolt. It was
1935 or 6, and there was nothing
anyone could think to do but live on.

Pocket Gopher

Not the one that may, or may not
be in your pocket the morning after
some hard drinking. I mean the sand rat
you seldom see, except for those little
mounds of earth its hindfeet push back
when it's burrowing. Once way down,
the dirt goes in the large pouches
on either side of its toothy mouth.

I trapped one once, tried to keep it
for a pet. At first, it seemed happy
in my hands. Come on, hurry up, it said,
I'm really starving. Or, I'm not a homeless
pup now, whee! But then, unaccountably,
its eyes just went, as if faded by sun,
and it grew thin, lost its golden color.

When it stopped talking one May evening,
I decided to let it go, from which time on
my life stayed exactly the same, the way
the sand rat always leaves neat little
piles of earth that are exactly the same.
They may not look the same, but they are.

Cremation Thoughts

The box of ashes the funeral home signs over to us
is surprisingly heavy. We pass it back and forth in
a bewildering tempo. The ashes seem to spread before
the mind's eye. It's as if the air changed, and all
you believe had vanished. If you take them to the
White Tank Mountains where she wanted to rest,
the funeral director says, Make sure no one's around.
The first policeman who sees you will arrest you, it's
the law. We nod and help each other on with our coats.

The little tree we stop by seems so bare you tie a bit
of yellow ribbon to a branch. We let Dad take the box
by himself to the gulley beyond, watch him broadcast
like some Johnny Appleseed. It's normal, I suppose,
to wonder what we'll want to do with our remains, but
this hardly seems the time to say anything out loud.

Some people approach now, coming energetically along
the trail through the narrow canyon, the great rock
walls rising around them. They stop right past us,
talking excitedly together in what might be Navajo.
They're quite out of breath. Mom's emphysema, that's
not what it was like at the end, I know. It wanted
something from her she couldn't give. Dying is such
hard work, she said at last. I started to drift,
the slow ride down past cactus having a hard time
of it this year. At the house, I wake up in a fit,
with a crazy resolve to be buried in what's left of me.

Marbles in Moline

—for AC

At home, after shooting marbles
all Saturday afternoon in the alley,
I dumped a pocketful of white bibbies,
striped plasters and bullies on my desk.
My shooter, a blood-alley, painted with
streaks of red, always came out last.
I put them all back in their stable,
the bottom of an old Chinese Checkers
box under my bed, the shooter facing
all the others from its own corner.

When arcing away from between my cocked
thumb and crooked forefinger, it knocked
its share of plebes out of the circle.
But I could tell it preferred solitude
to the most brilliant games, dressed
in its creamy reds it looked more like
a tiny Mars than any real sight on earth.
I'm not sure what I was doing then was living.

When Borges asked me 50 years later what
I remember most liking as a child, growing
up in Illinois, *Exactly*, he whispered, Tell
me *exactly*, I believe he had all the snow
and ice in mind, but I blurted right out:
Wiping that shooter coated with dust as clean
as I could, Sir. He tipped his head back, and
there was that horrible red at the bottom of
his eyes sliding into view. Hand me my cane, he said.

Dog Eye

It's the marble with a single scratch or crack,
the stare that never blinks. After the fever,

they shaved my head, by now the wig is gray.
Whether you're happy or unhappy in this life,

don't keep on about it, kneel down, hunch if
you have to, but pick off all the other mibs

till winter comes around again, it's check-up
time once more —the X-ray technicians are

brusque, even rude, the way I like it now —
extremes alone are logical. The next morning,

the all-clear sounds again for another year.
It occurs to me that the instinct that keeps

me in the game, for which I'm ill adapted,
is more reasonable than the reason that wouldn't.

Black Widow at the Kitchen Window

I'm doing the dishes and there it is, wholly black
out of the blue (I can't see the spot yet, which I've
read is red) — like feelings hardly ever allowed to
surface. If we could speak, we'd both speak at once.

There's as much difference between us and ourselves,
and ourselves and others, Montaigne says somewhere,
a serious charge to bring against God's creatures.
The widow seems to pause a moment, as if waiting for
Miss Muffet — I'm your boot-boy for now, I offer,
and stand content to let the dishwater run cold.

Sun's setting, I want to be free for any exchanges,
but more silence makes me shift my gaze to the tree
out back, bent down to the briars from last night's
storm; things that crawl on the ground have gone
in search of things that bloom in the air — some
of us to do the killing, others the grunting. It's
a pity the spider can't talk, I think, but it can:

Damn it all, I was ordered to live this way, period!
She makes a delicate, hairy-backed, sleight of hands'
sort of motion, as if washing off sin by habit. I think
I'd better have more witnesses, call the children to see,
but she's gone of course when they come by. They think
I'm fooling. My feeling's not so much embarrassment as
restlessness — that I've been a traitor to the spider's
true nature, by wanting her to be there by mere command.

Shift the Rod

The moment the bait hits the water, press
the rod's butt against your stomach, use

the last three fingers of either hand to
grasp the grip above the reel. With thumb

and index finger, pinch the line — all this
to free the other hand to operate the reel.

There's really no other way, believe me. It
will take you a long time to recover from

losing the fish of your life. The time I did,
I see it was based on a chain of errors. I

was one of those kids you couldn't tell a thing.
I'd scratch you off, kick you with an eye, have

a crazy fit if I felt like it. All my helpless
father could say was, You think you're so perfect.

And have nothing to do with me between vacations.
I finally woke up, that August on Bearskin Lake.

Dad just sat there with the oars idling, when
my fish struck, didn't even go for the net, not

that I'd have asked him. Never occurred to me
he'd ever become my teacher till we both saw

what I'd failed to hook: a musky with a head
so large I fell backwards into the water when

it came out of church, saying a prayer for me.
I remember the spot exactly, can take you anytime.

Day Owl

— for David

Short-eared, diurnal. You'd worry
it might starve its way to extinction.

But then it rolls those serious eyes,
nods that head, and it can do anything

nocturnal owls can do and then some.
Sometimes, at dawn or dusk, they meet

over a mouse, enjoy a jolly meal together
in a clear patch, turning darker or lighter

depending on the bills' tick. Ten minutes
into the dark, though, the day owl's off,

like someone who's recollected something
pleasant, and with marked courtesy invites

its counter-part to follow. But the all —
nighter shrugs its feathers, turns to me

instead, hoots, Where *did* she come from?
I allow as how I'll find out, follow her

deeper and deeper into the woods, night's
its darkest now, a reason for lasting....

The Empty Schoolroom

A few sparrows assemble in the rafters.
From the shadow on the flag a stripe detaches

and moves into isolation on the dusty blackboard.
Lincoln's left eye seems to stray. Our books

say aloud, Then we shall serve the Lord our God.
What a terrible line of poetry, The Frost Reader

replies, and the custodian comes along, plays
chopsticks on the piano, closes it up again.

And no one squeals or shouts, laughs or claps
her hands as if carried away. And no one asks,

How much did the grocer give Mrs. Clark back if
she gave him $10 for 3 cans of soup; 33¢ each?

The front door's open, but no one's there to survey
the wide space that becomes the road, as we've done

who pledged allegiance and were carried so far away,
single passengers forgiven our simple answers.

Never

Chinese pheasants used to be
all around the farms out here.

Brought from China, we suppose.
16-18 inches high, 2 lbs. or so,

red cone, red breast, heavy neck
feathers, honk like geese and we

used to love to eat it now and then,
till it turned up in Ming Lan's story.

Sent from China, she's in town now
on a hunt for a new life — her

parents having forked over $10,000
to spring her, we hear. She's not

told us the worst that's happened.
We head out to Miller's for home

made ice-cream, sit at the picnic
table behind the store, and while

we lick and smile, watch the field
beyond for any sign of life. When I

spot the bird, tell Ming it's hers,
she shakes her head, watches it

peck along. You're the ones who
eat it, she says, We never did.

The One Above

See the cheap cedar pencil behind
my grampa's ear? He's in his grocery
on 11th & Galina, next to the abandoned
Coptic church, his eyes looking as if
they've been dry a long time. Ringing
up your items, he'll stop at vespers
and matins only he can hear, light
a candle if you nod, All right, then,
he'd point at me, stocking shelves, He
won't be hearing the sounds of our fathers
much, now that the church is gone, alas.
And I don't have time to teach him.
His prayers will have to reach the Lord
on their own. You mean The One Above?
Mrs. Haba says, Lord's too simple a word
for The One Above, and now she's pointing
up, her finger shaking. With one of those
grim looks I only see him give once
a year, grampa says, more softly now,
When we reach the end of the journey,
we'll need to shorten things a little.

Picasso's Woman with One Breast Exposed

I was so afraid of her up there
over my crib, I couldn't sleep.
I realize my parents meant no harm
hanging her over me, a sort of aging
Penthesilea, looking over the infant
Achilles, I heard my father say and
my mother took his hand for withdrawing.
I bunged my mouth with a bit of thumb,
turned away to live. She'd bend down,
coughing, her downcast eye fluttering.

Now, past the middle of my own life,
I've known women who have lost theirs
to cancer, toast them with a midnight
glass of water by my bedside: Aunt
Jessie, Gramma Bess from Chicago, Al
Jordan's mother, Miss Joseph my algebra
teacher, my father's drugstore clerk,
and sweet, sweet Lila, a friend's wife,
who taught us all about carrying on.

Some nights I get up and walk a little
in the direction they've gone. If that
seems helpless, it is, oh I know it is.
And when I get ill, I write nothing but
some nonsense to another woman I barely
know who's had hers removed. Lately, I
figure that if I keep after my wife and
daughter to check theirs, I'm doing *one*
thing, but of course I can't imagine
the possibility of being interfered
with like that. Something I've never
dreamt about, something to fester.

Damfoolskis

Sometimes we wished Uncle Abe'd been just
Mr. Buttinski, or even Allrightski, the thing
of it was, he didn't stop there. When the cards

were dealt, the pennies stacked, the vane of
inclination swung in the direction of family
forgiveness, he upped and started in on Dad.

Sure, that bad deal left us at the mercy of
our wants, but Dad never meant any harm, even
let me break my piggybank to invest. We'd drive

round and round the land the family compound
was to be built on, later the teapot would be set
to boiling. Gramma said, Hurry, I can't last.

Uncle Abe fell through the first window into
the basement hole, months of neck collars followed.
Not to mention that scary leg brace he'd snap off,

chase me with till Mom gave him what for. Lately,
Abe's stopped living altogether, the family's been
busted up, a couple of us aren't even in the States

much but Abe keeps the stupid cards coming: If it
weren't for your Pop, we'd all be together and cozy.
Hell, I keep writing back, Dad couldn't know it was

a scam, no one saw dark signs, we all had a part in
drawing curtains so the sunlight fell from our dumb
faces and besides, Dad's paid enough by now, Abe,

compared with which our troubles are a bunch of grapes.
P.S.: Dad's at the sanitarium, keeps hearing the Lord say,
Go, befriend other families, till one appreciates you at last.

Feather Crown

Superstition has it that feathers
in our pillows form a crown when
we're dying, and it's no lie —
when gramma died, we found them
tightly woven, surprisingly heavy,
a ball we used to play games with,

though when I tell you this in some
whispered hush, putting on a reverent
face, you almost laugh, What else do
you think they'd do in there, under her
head? A looney schoolgirl made that up!

Understanding Poetry

— for IA & GE

The last time I saw him, that summer we were visiting at his villa near Salzburg, one of us screwed up her courage to ask for his autograph. He'd just come up from the cellar, insisting on bringing up one more case of Coke, quick to point out he could still get it in the old bottles. Only if you have a ball-point pen, Fräulein Sally, I love writing with them, he said, wiping the sweat from his face with the cowboy handkerchief I'd given him on my last visit.

Pen in hand, he beckoned us to follow him out to the veranda. We went along like schoolchildren on a walk to the museum. From a bell jar on the sideboard, he carefully rolled away one long, thin cigarette from the arched pile — Turkish, I realized, from his early poems — the way a player plays Pick-Up-Sticks. We formed a half-circle around him, Sally stepping slightly forward. He licked his lips, wet the pen and wrote his name with a tiny flourish next to the Turkish script on the cigarette. There, he said, handing it to Sally, Now let's sit outside in the garden and listen to your air-force on its way over our Alps. We coaxed him into reading one more poem with the last of his voice that day — he'd had surgery on his vocal chords, but the radiation had gone well, he assured us. Besides, my doctor likes me to read, stretches things down there. When a jet slashed past, he paused mid-sentence, There, that's enough, your people want the last word, see you next year perhaps — did you like the sandwiches? I may have some dark beer next time.

Christmas, the first of his cards came. Mein Lieber, has Sally smoked it up yet? I had to think to make the connection. Lordie, I thought, smoked it? Typical of you, Günter! Sally was still at school, so I called on the pretext of wanting to show her a certain book. I knew he wouldn't want me to ask her directly, so I sort of wondered aloud, What has ever happened to that autographed cigarette? I was hoping you'd ask, she said, Right there, on the mantle! Under a little glass bell, there it was! Fairly aglow, the signature alive, looking a little Turkish.

And so our correspondence started up in earnest. I wrote back, Dear G, nope, on the oldest postcard I could find, Not yet. And every three or four months, for the next year or so, he'd write, sometimes just, Yet? Once, the card said, Is it thin air, finally? I'd try to find out, write back, and on and on. Finally, Sally graduated, moved away — Dear G, I recall writing then, I'll have to save some money before I can check on the cigarette again. Sally's gone to China....

Günter's wife handed me the last card in our exchange, which never got sent. I'd come to visit, but he'd died a week before. I stared down hard at the tiny script: Lieber, I guess she never really understood my poems at all.

II

The Child in Us

Not the Sunday the Japanese bombed Pearl Harbor,
not the Sunday I broke my nose playing in the park,
certainly not the Sunday I accidentally locked sis
in the screen porch and something behind her caught
fire. Not even the Sunday dad got blood poisoning
planing wood in the basement. The draft said 4-F.

It was the Sunday Don Hutson, speeding on toward
the goal line, veered at the last moment for an upright
and reeling himself around the goalpost with one arm,
the defending back sailing on past toward the stands,
did catch Cec Isbell's perfect pass with his other arm.

From my child's point of view at the time, the War
sent back only cracked sound, the whole nose business
was suspicious, my parents thought I set that fire
but I loved my sister, I wished my father buried
as a hero, but with that catch, the artistry of it,
a way of thinking about the past presented itself.

The Grizzly Bear and the Chicken Flip

are what my parents say they danced
in the Grand Salon on Meinecke Street.

Why is it the dances have changed so
much? father wonders, and mother lifts

the veil from my eyes so I can see
their world for what it really was.

I don't want the corpses of dances
about me either, I think of saying,

but it isn't likely to make a difference.
They're hiding away in their little house

in Momence. You don't think it's too ugly
here, do you, doesn't smell too much of cat,

does it? they wonder. I wish I hadn't brought
the nursing home up now, look at them for what

they've managed to become, and suggest getting
out the old records one more time   they protest

of course but underneath have waited for this
moment: father holds a hand out, mother struggles

to her feet with her cane, and next thing I know
they're doing beautifully. Not exactly restored,

not young again, none of that crap, but rising up
over the agony of facing death in a little while,

way past appeals for sympathy. There's even
some cunning when they flip right past my chair,

the sort of cunning people show others
as if others had first shown it to them.

No One Coughs in My House

Everyone going to America in the 20s was told
to come straight to my house on Milwaukee Avenue,
Libby Kahn will take care of you! And I took

all of them in of course, she says, Sometimes
for months. I made the best mustard plasters —
all those coughs! And chests so thin you could

see right through to their brave little hearts.
She looks astonished for a moment, like some
harried animal, her eyes straying from the faces

of the other women in the beauty parlor at the Home
for the Aged. What's your name again, Dear? I think
she says to me — I steady my hand on my mother's

arm, who tries to straighten up in her wheelchair,
under the hairdryer. Why, we're the Garbers from Vilna,
originally, I tell her, And I bet one cousin or other

had some of your fine chicken soup back then....
Her eyes glisten, Yes, I knew a Garber, it means
tanner you know, nice fellow. I gave him what

I could, along with the rest. The more they have
the better they will live, I thought, and time
passed on. The One Above came to see they were
happy. Now what did you say your name was, Dear?

Calliope

Steamers going by downriver used to have them,
all that steam fueling the pipes. Big circuses

had two, usually the last wagons in the parade.
When we settled down in school, Miss Bartz held

the picture book over her head, "At some point
a plain old-fashioned steam piano was named for

the mother of Orpheus," she said, "I suppose
because the inebriated player was quite intelligent,

a fan of the great myths." I wrote all that down.
"Nothing's better than a sit-down chat with your

calliope," grampa used to say, "Now I'm going to
quote Mozart a little wrong," he joked and floated

some notes far out beyond my ear. We went to find
him a home as close as possible, near the end, and

tried to get the old tunes going again, but the notes
fell apart on his lips. The last circus has long since

gone from these parts, and I'm a little sleepy myself,
come to think. Out back, in a shed we built for grampa's

calliope, it seems to be puffing away. I'm not so sure
it's just the fog. If you open the curtains, the grass

is smooth and blue, the circus poster grampa brought
from Budapest just starting to come free of its tacks.

Now That Dad Is Gone

She was her usual self at supper, "Pass...
we'd say. "Heavens," she might answer, or
"I think I'll lie down before our game."
My brother did the dishes, I got the board
out, found some dice, then we took our walk
around the block while she changed her clothes.

I remember my brother saying the smoother the surface,
the less friction between things, which quickly led to
the times she would help us with our algebra, Suppose
the boy is pulling the cart with a force of 10 lbs.,
Suppose we can draw two lines at right angles, starting

from the point the cart started.... Henry laughed before
I could. Do you think it's Alzheimer's? I realize she's
getting up there, but she still calls Henry by my name,
the way she always has. I doubt she has other visions,
nothing in her is enigmatical. She's flooded with life.

Yes, but who *is* she? Henry stops, Who *is* she? His cry
goes down the street, lit by evergreens. And the gate
is open when we return. She's there, leaning in the door.
I was sleeping so soundly, she says, But then I just
woke up, just like that. I wanted to be with my sons.

“Like the Beams That Make a Tent over the Church at Night”

—Virginia Woolf

But they were searchlights, and it was war.
When we think of agonies like hers, no one

should have done all she did. Leonard would
forget the lemon, she to cook the haddock after

one of those days, conceding almost everything,
conceding nothing. In my dream she's a peasant

in a shabby coat, throwing crusts to some swans
along the bank, refusing to fall in with the plan

to drown this time. It would be nice, I think, if
she were still alive, agreed to speak to us, with

our pathological thirst for the right words, and
I imagine no one ever finished her sentences.

Reading back to front, I come across this entry,
it's Wednesday, 6 September, 1939: “No raids yet.

Poland being conquered & then — we shall be
attended to.” I suspect our predisposition for

insanity is for our own amusement.... Earlier,
1936 now, Kipling's dead and the King's dying.

How *is* the Empire? he is said to have said with
his final breath. And was told it was doing fine.

Fried Shirt

You've got your fried shirt on, gramma would say and
we loved the way she said it, fingered all the pearly
buttons before she'd put her hands to her hips, step
back for one more look. Just to visit me! she shook
her head and grinned that old-world way, lopsided.
She'd entered life with very little hope, in Senice,
which till a while ago was filled with Russian tanks,
though the church on the square is still the same.
I don't know what I would or could have said to her,
if she were alive to hear about my visit right before
the dam broke, and Russia wasn't Russia anymore. Maybe
that, roaming the streets, the people still seemed as
friendly as she would often recall, even in their little
wretched houses. Puffs of wind deposit dust on your shirt.

She went to the seamstress school for girls in town,
one building I asked to visit. They gave her an iron
when she graduated, which she used till her dying day,
a universe away. The school's still there, all right,
but there's a barbed wire fence around it now that won't
come down for a while, and some sort of guard at the gate
who couldn't understand the little Czech I know. I toyed
with the idea of showing him her picture, leaning on a table
over the hot iron, perplexed. She didn't have to keep ironing
if she didn't want to. We'll never have a quiet world again,
she used to say, Never in a thousand thousand thousand years.

The Farkleberry Tree

In Texas, in open woods, the dry, sandy soil
sprouts them like so many beans. The best way
to get up one's with a rope around your neck,
Uncle Ross used to say, when I begged him to
boost me up to the first branch and he wouldn't.

Later, he came clear, That's where the body hung
for a whole week before anyone would cut it down.
The office for the dead was finally read and they
dug a grave right beside the thick trunk. When
it rained, it was the place your feet would stick

in the soft mud. Uncle's near the end of his breath
now, and we say it together, Let's mark that grave
properly.... The stone we find is shaped like a horse's
head, and all we do is chalk in an eye, for the pony
someone slapped so the rope could take to jerking —
One of those local trials, Uncle said at last, and
though I was only ten, I should have tried to stop them.

As How

She said *as how* it was her opinion,
and you'd not risk saying, What a
dumb pleonasm.... After all, she
shoots her own gun. Just last week
we heard *as how* there was a quarrel
between her and him — once upon
a time there was a fairy who made
birds and bees lovers, trees and
flowers too that last as long as
there's light for all the shadows.

Somehow, she'd not thought all
the world would be so dark, quiet
after someone dies, the little
trail of life that led in her
direction, but seldom traveled,
as how, she said later, it was
very steep and here and there
great boulders lay across it.

Feather Merchant

If you cried in grampa's presence, he'd kiss away
your tears, make you a nice feather pillow, ease

your head down, sing to you softly. After you got over
childhood, he pulled you to the corner bank, opened a

savings account with a dollar in your name. I remember
the moment when this all could have gone so differently.

I'd had a good breakfast, done some chores, walked
the dog, and there was grampa at the radio with his

one good ear when I looked in. The President's declared
war, he said, And the Bears are up by seven. So we threw

in with the Packers, I recall. Don Hutson came from nowhere,
and the Pack was back. It's not clear what happened next

in that life, but when I broke my nose, landed in
the hospital with strep to boot, there was grampa,

holding up a single feather: Blow it up toward the light,
he said, You will see the blood that has been left behind.

The Widows of Sun City

Mrs. Colbarth gets up at 3 a.m. sometimes. She steps
into the shower with the water off, pulls on lace
stockings, pours a shot of cranberry juice, taps
the cat back to sleep and before hosing down her drive
moves the Le Baron and the golf cart across the street,
their lights still on when I'm out at six to walk the dog.

Others are up now, there's Mrs. Herrick pulling her drapes,
waving me past, and Mrs. Jessen has a cup of coffee ready,
but calls me Ray and thinks I'm the mailman. That's a good
idea, she says, To have a dog for other dogs along your route!
Mrs. Childress is already half way up her grapefruit tree,
twisting the ladder so I worry. She's still something to behold,
tosses me a couple, says there'll be more if the Salvation Army
won't come for the rest. Used to help with the harvest, she says.

There are more and more FOR SALE signs up, it's been a
hard year.
The obituaries fall behind. I used to make donations to the right
charities, but my own pension's not doing so well, sorry to say.
More strokes this year, I hear, less cancer and heart. Sometimes
I forget you can see the White Tank Mountains over there, the
saguaro on the peaks some of my visitors take for TV antennas!
If they want a little outing, I pack a picnic for the trail to
the waterfall, ask if we can take Miss Kathleen along. She calls
herself Mrs. Right, for never having married wrong. When we
honk,
she throws open the door. It's mid-morning, a hot wind's going.
She's got her huge straw hat balanced on her lovely hair and I
mean to court her some time down the gravel road, but not now.

Where Do You Suppose He'd Go Now?

We get cards from him for a bit, tiny little scribbles.
Then, at the end, nothing. I get up from my chair,
sit down again, pour more brandy, tilt my head back,
pinch my eyes, go back for a moment to that night
so long ago. His eyes were glazed from watching TV.
He walked past me into the kitchen: Remember that
old model airplane we made together when I came home
from the war? he said. A Zero, with those red circles
like cheap suns on the wings. Quite a plane, though.
You always split the balsa when I said, Now stick that
damn pin in right there, there! But I made a mess of
the paper job, kid, never did like glue. I recall, Dad.

I loved it when we were finally finished, only to realize
we'd forgotten to hook up the rubberband! Had to break back
inside, nothing much, just a little slit with the blade.
We ran to the yard but it didn't do much, lost a wing or two.
Dad pointed to the garbage can and we went on to something
 else,
something that's gotten us up to now. So when he calls to wish
me Happy Birthday from some place he won't name, I start in
on him, Goddammit, you won the fucking war, Dad, came back
honest, tried your best. Remember? It's me who broke the wood.

Children and Rocking Chairs

Have you noticed, it's the first
piece of furniture children go to
even in a crowded room? They stand
there a while, pondering aloud how
it works in that double-echo voice,
their feet fixed as iron. Then they
smile, extend a finger, put some
muscle into the notion. The chair
moves! Half a hand goes to work.

Occasionally, you see them sitting
in the rocker in the corner, quiet,
a frown on their brow, letting the
small doll fall from their lap, gazing
toward the sky with closed eyes, arms
crossed, the world below made one and
if you dab at their eyes, they will
cry out, but the next thing you know
they're running about again, greedy,
their restlessness returned. You wish
them all the joy they can ferret out,
see J.F.K. resting his bad back in
that white highchair someone fastened
rockers to so it could creak and creak.

Chalk the Rabbit

I stole some chalk, drew arrows down the sidewalk,
but you never found me. I admit I never did tell you
where I was headed, would that have helped? Remember
the game we used to play? There you'd be at the end
of 100 rabbits, it seemed, giggling behind a tree,
happy to be found at last. We skipped for lemonade.

Well, I'll be going, I said another time, bit my lip.
You wanted to chime in, or so I thought, lifted those
eyes, the library turned gloomy. I excused myself, to
look up something like "goose step," for my thesis,
but kept right on going past definition — an 1806
training exercise for young recruits; teaches balance.

The war came later, one thing led to another, we married
different people, moved away and wrote just once. You
included a picture, your two girls hanging on to your
legs for dear life. I couldn't write back; tried calling.
We both spoke at once, a language never spoken since.

III

Van Gogh's Cyclist

Someone else painted it, come to think!
But if Van Gogh had, the boy would make

it to a tall house on a hump of ground,
be safe in a little bed in the corner,

the bicycle leaning against a shed, a sort
of sexual object, waiting for the drawbridge

to settle back over the lazy creek. It's
way past dark now, the boy's fast asleep,

feeling just a slight ache from the past.
In the distance, the lamp from a boat flickers.

Babblers

are what they call dogs that just bay, throw
their tongues around without picking up any scent.
Ours are perfect examples, but we'd never think
of not taking them along to hunt. As soon as I
get a good shot in, I'll come right back, you'd
best stay with the mutts, Dad says. The moon
comes up, and I find myself as alone as ever.

Dad goes through the bushes without making a sound.
I empty the shells out of my gun and sit down between
Harold and Harry, pet their skulls. When I was allowed
to name them, I don't know what came over me. Dad just
swallowed but wouldn't ask me to reconsider. It's what
I've always liked about him — he hands you something,
then stands back. That was my childhood, but now that
I'm married, it won't work for me. My love's a burden
for my children. I feel like crying sometimes. The worst
is when they press the palms of their hands to their faces.

All I've done is look at them the way you do at something
you expect to lose one day. A little way off, to be sure.
You're just sitting there and they don't come back or even
call out, and maybe it's just the other side of the bushes.

The Digdee Owl

Whooping from the cedar, near the house,
or is it the chimney now? — wonder who's

the next to die, unless the legend's got
it wrong. Isn't nothing but a screech owl,

Uncle Abe says, and tries to whistle Hound
Dog. I'm about to plunge into the pond out

back, when I feel what you do when there's
someone behind you you can't see — just a

sensation, mind you. At dusk the whoops start
coming up again, so I look the screech owl up:

such fat thighs, the muscular, pink tongue!
Belongs in church with us, holding a candle

at Vespers, singing *Turris Eburnea.* I hope
its nest is not too near, Uncle says after

a week of steady whoops, We'd have to search
it out, look for remains — he's given up on

his screech-owl theory. The sound's louder now,
none of us moves — it's no sound to fool with,

something hurrying toward you, starting in
at the ear, moving to the medulla, burning.

Hairy Woodpecker

Can you tell me how the bird out back
got its name? It doesn't have a single
hair on its body. It haunts our orchard.

If the apple trees had oil, we'd be rich
from all the wells it's sunk into them,
soon its body is swollen with insects

like a drowned man. But then it hop-steps
so fast to the next hole it can barely
keep its feet. The precise spot it now

stands I call Little Vilna, in memory of
gramma who picked such a tree and such
a bird before the Germans came.

Egg Roast

— for MS

It's Easter in Romania again,
more exactly, in the plain of
the Black Sea, where eggs are
cooked with mud, roasted in a
fire no one sits around to sing
any sort of song, because at
this moment, people are about
to step off a ferry, confused
and lonely in their own land,
and the dreadful swelling on
their heads just won't go down.

Here Cossie, Cossie

Old cows know it's just the calf we're calling,
whose liver's more agreeable to us, interests your
whole mind, even if it doesn't look as if it might,

in the meatcase, glistening under its price-tag. John,
fascinated by attention, goes to stroke its lean neck.
Why, it has a pulse, just like ours, he says, not one to

indulge in deep meditation at the edge of a lonely field.
Usually, I can't think of eating to live without growing
aggressive. In the course of the meal, please let's have

none of your lively imaginations without recalling your
blessings: Some have meat and cannot eat, and some have
none that want it.... For now, let's just pet the calf,

dream of the future of vegetarianism, weak in the joints
if we lose track of protein, root of all powerlessness,
alongside our capacity to despise ourselves, Helen adds.

Look how clumsy the calf is, its head a shade too bulky
for its body, its tail not yet able to swat every fly,
the moisture of its eyes like water squeezed from a sponge.

The Requiem Shark

— for A

Said to exist chiefly
in tropical waters, where,
contrary to belief, depths
can be gloomy, full of
unnerving sadness, as if
a geological error and
diving down Nietzsche comes
to mind: not how one soul
comes closer to another,
but how it moves away,
tells about kinship.

We merely expect
a wallowing in pleasure
when it turns a cold shoulder,
on the born side of creation,
as beside it human swimmers
do not seem to have matured:

it is the most alarming
of our qualities, while
the shark's bloodless gaze
calls forth piety, then nausea.

Fool Hen

Ruffed grouse, that often sit
by the side of the road, nodding.
If you want something to stew,
they'll be out there to harvest.

When I was sent to vacation with
Uncle Ross, he tried to teach me
to knock them out with his whip,
save a mess. I never did get good

at it, but I've never been hungry
in my life. Just let me watch one
more time, I'd beg, so he shook
the whip till the sheaf fell and

all the tails turned into a whole
regiment. Thing of it is, he said,
You can't be afraid of God at the
moment you strike. Just remember

to pray over supper, even if you
don't get the words exactly right,
should fool the hen into thinking
it's been twice blessed. My lips

ice up when I bite in, Get through,
you fool, please get through this
in a hurry, I mutter to myself while
Uncle Ross always takes seconds.

Visiting Robert Francis with My Son

We ask about the crayon-poems on the desk.
There's quite a heap of them, you can't take
your eyes away. Oh, he says, I try to write
one every day now. I surely like Crayolas,
doesn't everyone? He reaches over but knocks
the orange to the floor. Don't bother, please,
I'd like to fetch it, he seems to say and takes
many moments to lower his arthritic shape down
notch by notch to the knee, by hanging on tight
with both hands to the desk. We look away while
he takes many more moments getting back up —
There it is, he says, Now I can do another one
in orange! We wave off an offer to make tea.

It's been the usual sweet time everyone reports
having in his cheerful company, from the walk
about the yard to the request for a photo with
him standing between those two hubcaps he's
rescued from an abandoned car and driven into
the grass before the door. We're worried we're
tiring him, but he says, Any last questions before
you go? Well, my son wonders, taking in all of
the woodenness to the place, worrying about fire
of course, Do you keep all your poems here, sir?
No, my boy, Francis winks, They're all in a nice
safety deposit box in the town bank, thank you.

Only for an Hour

On the way to the Dead Sea scrolls,
the bus driver stops at the sea itself
for some facts: You probably know its
average depth is 1,080 feet, he says,
But around shore you can't drown so
I encourage you to take a dip. Even
if you can't swim, you'll still look
pretty nice bobbing around! Ah, you
know about the 85 million pounds of salt!
No monsters though, so nothing can happen.
Please be back in an hour, bye bye, now.

We rent bathing trunks and towels, cast
off, wave to each other from our various
positions. Fear of falling through is only
a fancy now. More and more, we're preoccupied
with praying for other things when it happens:
as if from nowhere, I swear, Jesus suddenly appears,
kisses our parched lips, puts his soft hands on
our knees, brings himself to a perfect headstand
on our chests. Tell me the whole truth, he says
in some distress, When you entered my lake,
did you know it would only be for an hour?

Beaver Poison

Musquash root, or spotted cowbane,
so deadly I'm surprised it's never
been used in a murder mystery. Grows
out past the beaver lodge, where
the yellow pond lily wavers, and
if you're foolish enough to taste
it, the only thing you'll be able
to recall is its name before you
head for heaven, the Indians say.

Then you'll be very very hungry for
a second, your tongue will harden,
your fingers open, lose their hold,
then it'll be over and done with,
just like that, before the beavers
paddle by on their backs to look,
who are not used to seeing humans
wash up against their lodge. They
close their eyes so that your big
black boots won't frighten them,
so that their faces won't wrinkle
all at once, so that the root will
grow again, though seen and eaten.

Good-Gods

Noisy when the sun comes up over the swamp,
they'll be up in the hardwoods, cack-cacking,
or puck-pucking, like any respectable woodpecker.

It takes a certain mind to see divinity in that,
because inch for pileated inch it's the greatest
ruffian on earth, grampa says, Its banquets end
in a fight, it never loses to the crows or jays
a few branches over, hear them whimpering now?

If you look close, they can cross their legs as
elegantly as your gramma, sitting down in the chair
on the porch. What's so fine in that dreary song?

she says, when I direct her attention to the side
of the cypress: it's faintly visible now, a sovereign
prince in a dressing gown, suddenly afoot in the midst
of our petty, obscure lives, and if it hears rumors
of its devilness, its fury fixes the distance between
the good God and the bad, or something like that....

Bumblebee Duck

It's small and moves its wings very fast,
as the name suggests. Be that as it may,
the story goes that long ago, as the first

tenderness burst forth on earth, reached
human lips, formed the basis of our genes,
the birds and bees were mere apparitions.

If we looked at them, they didn't come closer.
Those of us who managed to look more intensely
began to make connections: I don't know that

animal personally, but if you just look how
fast its fins are stirring, why, the air's
thick with hums! Pity it can't talk, is all.

Who said, The most exclusive love for anything
is always a love for something else as well? So
we go on declaring we're fond of one thing while

we make our peace with something else. Perhaps
this just brings out the sacred in us, at best,
or merely excites bodily passions innocent of

bodily desire. Never mind, the duck doesn't look
too troubled at the possibilities. It swims past
easily, its eye turbid, its brown breast quiet.

Fence Mouse

In some places, they call it striped
or spotted prairie squirrel, chipmunk
even, but here in Ohio, where it's always
on a fence, just about ready to tumble over,
like milk turning sour, we like fence mouse.

My German neighbor says it's from *fenzmaus*,
or something like that. Often we trade shadows
when I'm out mowing the yard, and when mine
falls on it, it looks up suddenly to see
what's passing. You can see by its ears

it's listening too. Finally, it shakes
its head, scratches a shoulder, and its
whole body comes alive again, suffused
with purifying movement which, like sun,
makes everything seem much more decent.

Sunt Lacrimae Rerum

The long gray trail of tears,
running from our eyes, rising
and falling illogically, when we
push back into our chairs so we don't
fall on our knees. We want to run but
our legs will not obey us, to run
from what we have seen and done.

Our tears fly higher and higher,
so high the rope slackens, and
they fly even higher and higher.

The faster they fly, the nearer
they come to the sun, which calls
out to Virgil, They'll kill me yet,
but Virgil can only shrug a shoulder,
for he too is unable to stand up,
his hair combed back over his ears,
giving his face that fresh expression,
now that he has been able to direct
all the many many tears away from us.

STUART FRIEBERT has published eleven books of poems in English and German, as well as seven volumes of translations and five textbooks. His other work includes more than 30 articles, two prose memoirs, plus dozens of reviews and essays. He is widely known as the co-editor of Oberlin College Press: *Field;* the *Field* Translation Series; the *Field* Contemporary Poetry Series, as well as the co-editor of *The Longman Anthology of Contemporary American Poetry*, and *Models of the Universe: An Anthology of the Prose Poem.* Friebert has won an NEA Creative Writing Fellowship. He has taught at Oberlin College since 1961, where he directs the Oberlin Writing Program.